THE CHRISTIAN AND WAR

TOM SEALS

*As a medic having served with combat arms
while deployed, I felt a sense of hypocrisy
and difficulty articulating how to defend my
position as a maturing Christian. The text
summarizes in analytical faction how
a veteran may wield a weapon and simulta-
neously preserve life at war and return home
with honor morally and spiritually.*

Sergeant Jacob L. Schultz
Army National Guard
Operation Enduring Freedom

*I started my transition as a veteran in the
God's Word for Warriors course with Dr.
Seals. Dr. Seals created a safe environment
where we discussed tough topics that only
veterans would understand.*

Specialist Theresa Benner
U.S. Army
Operation Enduring Freedom

988

SUICIDE &

CRISIS LINE

Text **HOME** to 838255 to
connect with a volunteer
Crisis Counselor.

ATTRIBUTIONS
Interior Text Font: Minion Pro
Cover Design & Typesetting: Robbie W. Grayson III

ISBN: 979-8-8691-9378-0

BOOK PUBLISHER INFORMATION
Traitmarker Books
A Division of Traitmarker Media
www.traitmarkerbooks.com
traitmarker@gmail.com

Table of Contents

A Note from the Publisher

The publisher is providing this book and its contents on an "as is" basis and makes no representations or warranties of any kind with respect to this book or its contents and disclaim all such representations and warranties, including but not limited to warranties of mental healthcare for a particular purpose.

The content of this book is for informational purposes only and is not intended to diagnose, treat, cure, or prevent any mental/social condition or disease. This book is not intended as a substitute for consultation with a licensed practitioner. Please consult with a physician or healthcare specialist regarding the suggestions and recommendations made in this book.

Traitmarker Media, LLC

An Introduction to
God's Word for Warriors

Let me begin by sharing some basic facts about the military culture of today:

- Over 16 million veterans now reside in the United States, comprising 8.3% of the population.

- Many of these soldiers are not church goers—most veterans love Jesus, but not the church.

- Contrary to what most think, few vets are homeless, however, 35,574 veterans were homeless in the United States in January 2023 (HUD—Department of Housing and Urban Development).

- 10% of our veterans are women with personal needs tripling every year (U.S. Government Department of Labor).

What if you were...

- Deployed to a foreign land?

- Removed from symbols, institutions, and traditions you are most familiar with?

- In situations of continual danger, poverty, hopelessness, Godlessness, etc.?

- At a point in life brought on by military deployments when you felt abandoned by God?

This is the present situation with many of our veterans today. Following deployment(s), many return home and find difficulties in acclamation back into our society. Many of you are familiar with the Preamble to the Constitution: "We the people... provide for the common defense (sic)." Our nation's fundamental document speaks of a "shared sacrifice." What does this mean to you? It means that we are in this together— soldier and civilian alike!

Tom Seals

Bellevue, Tennessee | January 2024

Blessed are the peacemakers,
for they will be called
the children of God.

JESUS

Over the years I have engaged in serious study about what Scripture says about the Christian and war. This is a subject that has deeply divided the Christians since its beginning from the first century to this very day.

NO
WAR

This is a very complex question. I am *not* pro-war but I'm *not* a conscientious objector either. Is that a contradiction? I share this with you as a former Marine and one who is heavily involved with post-deployed veterans as a former faculty member in a College of Bible and Ministry, as a former Chaplain to student veterans, and currently all across this great nation of ours as the Director of God's Word for Warriors.

The quest for peace has always been one of our goals as Christians, yet this quest is always overshadowed by war and threat of war. War distorts lives and threatens the very survival of humanity. Nations fear the expansionist ambitions of neighboring nations. We stockpile weapons. Terrorists abound.

So, what does the Bible have to say about the Christian and war?

The question of war and Christian participation in it has been argued for more than two thousand years. With this in mind, we cannot do justice to the question of the Christian and war without speaking of the Hebrew Scriptures, the New Testament, and the Ante-Nicene Fathers. But the scope of this argument is too much for this little book.

So, I will limit my remarks to what the Bible says about Christian combatants by highlighting the New Testament teachings and insinuations on this subject. Of course, this will involve a word or two from time to time from both the Old Testament and the Ante-Nicene Fathers.

God commanded in the Old Testament, "You shall not kill." Jesus repeats the command in the Sermon on the Mount. But does this settle the issue? What about the Old Testament law, "Whoever sheds man's blood, by man shall his blood be shed, for in the image of God he made man"?(Genesis 9:6)

Apparently, this gives men, acting collectively (the state), the right to administer capital punishment and designate the individuals to carry this out!

God instructs the Israelites in some instances to form armies and kill their enemies. Why did God use nations to carry out justice and judgment, even against his own people? Does He prohibit Christians from engaging in war under any circumstance?

Old Testament Israelites lived under an ethical system that condemned revenge, limited self-defense, and encouraged loving fellow-Jews and foreigners, as true of the ethical system for New Testament believers.

For example, what the priest and Levite did in Jesus' Samaritan parable was contrary to the Mosaic Law (Luke 10:30-37). Paul even quotes from the Old Testament in Romans 12:19-21 about the importance of peace toward one's enemies.

Despite popular opinion, the Old Testament taught a personal ethic of non-retaliation and non-violence, along with the need for kindness to all in need. Yet the Old Testament does not see this as inconsistent in relation to its emphasis on the call for personal self-defense and just wars in defense of the nation.

What about the New Testament? John the Baptizer tells soldiers not to misuse their power, yet he says nothing about leaving the military (Luke 3:10-14).

And, in the Sermon on the Mount, Jesus taught love your neighbor; turn the
other cheek, give the cloak, etc.

The New Testament evidence is in-disubtable that Jesus encountered be-leivers who were in the Roman army. One was a centurion who sent the Jewish elders to ask Jesus to heal his servant who was about to die (cf. Matthew 8:5-13; Luke 7:1-10), about whom Jesus said: "I have not found such faith in all Israel."

Yet, Jesus never stated that military service on the part of these believers is contrary to God's will in these situations.

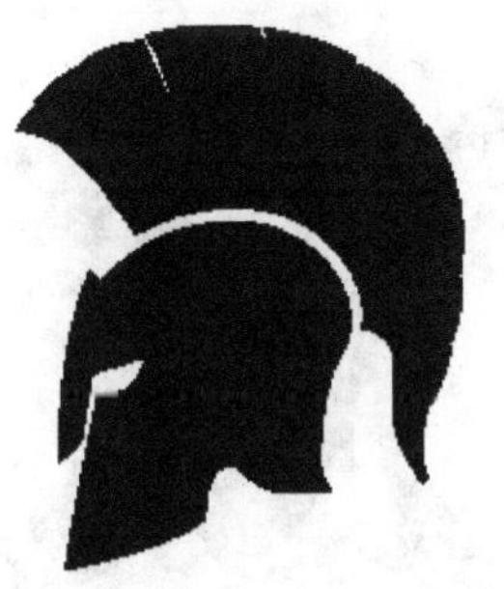

This same is true of the centurion at the foot of the cross who said of Jesus, "Surely he was [the, a] son of God" (Matthew 27:54). And to Cornelius, a centurion responding to the gospel as preached by Peter (cf. Acts 10). And of some within the palace guard when Paul speaks of his imprisonment there (Phil 1:13).

When Jesus gives the Sermon on the Mount, he was speaking to individuals, not the state. This sermon is a call to "personal" ethics, not national ethics.

So, the individual Christian must accept abuse and even death rather than deny Christ, yet must surely defend others as well as a nation against injustice. We should not avenge ourselves but are to live peaceably.

Paul put it in this way, "If possible, live at peace." (Romans 12:17-21)

However, if God gives the leaders of the state the right to resist evil through war, police force, etc., cannot the Christian support and join in the promotion of such justice?

Does the New Testament teach that Christians should passively bear verbal and physical abuse against themselves as well as others? Would doing so not allow continuing injustice and harm, thus setting aside the command to love (and all that "love" entails) one who is in a dangerous situation?

We may forgo resistance toward us individually, but if turning the other cheek leads to further abuse, it is no longer possible to live at peace if we do not stop the abuse. Did Jesus "turn the other cheek" when he was struck by the officer and replied, "Why do you strike me?" (John 18:23), or when he drove out the moneychangers in the Temple (cf. John 25)? And if one can do this as an individual, can't one also do this to promote the safety of a nation?

While on trial for his life, Paul responded to one of the authorities who ordered him to be struck for blasphemy, "God shall smite you, you whitened wall." (Acts 23:3) Paul's following apology was not that he didn't have the right to challenge his mistreatment, for this was according to the Law, but an apology for the sharpness with which he addressed the high priest.

It is obvious from the Ante-Nicene writings that Christians served in the Roman army. Pacifism was prevalent in the early church, however, this was not the only, or even dominant, view of this time period. The fact that the Ante-Nicene writings are concerned with this subject matter indicates that believers were serving in the military!

The evidence indicates that a Christian may resist injustice in any society and can serve in the military, police force, etc. However, it must be a just war or just cause that leads to such activity on the part of the Christian. I do not believe the Christian can fight in an unjust war, with the burden of proof of the righteousness of such resistance being on the individual Christian more than the state. However, if I dissent and choose not to engage in war, I must be willing to face the consequences of such dissent.

I recognize the right of those who refuse to participate in war because they believe such participation would violate their understanding of Jesus' pacifism. This does not mean they cannot serve their nation, however, for there are opportunities to serve in organizations such as the Peace Corps, Vista, as a corpsmen, etc.

Many of these pacifists turn the other cheek and place their lives in jeopardy because they refuse to bear arms for conscience's sake. However, does one have the right to place other lives in jeopardy because that person refuses to strike down evil?

We must also address the question: "Is war a moral evil?" I know of no one, General of the Army, veterans of wars, or present-day civil forces, who delight in war. It is a social evil and is of the devil (James 4:1-2).

However, it is not totally evil, or God would not have commanded it to be initiated by his own people.

In addition, history bears it out that some good has resulted from wars, in spite of the fact that most wars are both unnecessary and wrongfully motivated. I hear that war brings death instead of life. In just one example, did the call to war by the Allied Forces in WW II save thousands of Jews and others from ex-termination in Nazi Germany?

Scripture never calls war a moral evil, as such. Evil lies behind Hell, but it is morally necessary, as are jails and criminal courts. If war were morally evil, per se, would we read of Michael and his angels at war with the devil and his angels, or the military figures and symbols in Scripture? Would Miriam be characterizing God as promoting evil when she said, "The Lord is a man of war, the Lord is his name" (Exodus 15:3)?

Is it right for civil rulers to use coercive force? Can the state serve as a police force in order to save lives and promote peace when it fights against mobs destroying a city? If so, then is it right for Christians to be a part of that force for good? Or, has God designated one section of the society to do something as a matter of necessity and duty that the conscientious believer is forbidden to do for some think it involves sin?

Here we must spend a moment dis-cussing violence. This is a call for the understanding of the word *violence* and what such entails. We hear a lot about the issues of violence and nonviolence. Violence is often defined as "inflicting suffering on others, hurting or killing or forcefully taking advantage of others."

Yet the Old and New Testaments, speak of vengeance, retribution, and punishment, all of which can and often do involve violence. Paul, like Jesus, tells Christians to return good for evil, exhibit loving service to neighbors and enemies. Paul further teaches that personal vengeance is off-limits (Romans 12:19), and that God is the one to execute vengeance.

At times God will use governments to carry out his justice and this often entails force and violence.

So, if Christians find themselves in positions of governing authority, do they not then become servants of God's justice, rather than being personal vengeance-takers or promoters of personal violence?

The key word in all the discussions on the right of believers to bear arms is "peace-making." Again, Paul writes, "If it be possible as far as it depends on you, live at peace with everyone" (Romans 12:18 - NIV). Peace was at the very heart of conquering the Promised Land. The Mosaic Law states: "When you draw near to a city to fight against it, offer terms of peace to it. And if its answer to you is peace and it opens to you, then all the people who are found in it shall do forced labor for you and shall serve you. But if it makes no peace with you, but makes war against you, then you shall besiege it; and when the Lord your God gives it into your hands, you shall put all its males to the sword" (Deuteronomy 20:10-13).

In conclusion, what is my position in regard to the state and war? I do not have the competence to give omniscient guidance. We search in vain for any adequate, timeless statement of a "Just War." There are many doctrines of the just war which are the result of sincere spiritual insights and common sense. We differ on these.

However, two things we do agree on is that we cannot worship the state, any country, or any leader, other than Our Lord God. The second is that we are to love our neighbor as ourselves.

So, do you as a Christian particiapte in war? That answer is up to you.

TAKE
ACTION

We cannot violate our own conscience, neither can we judge another whose position concerning resisting evil differs from ours. We also have a responsibility to exercise the task of holding accountable those who commit unjust aggression against our neighbor while working for the restraint of personal vengeance. In addition, we can and must pray for our rulers and our nation and seek peace always as the first priority.

988

SUICIDE & CRISIS LINE

Text **HOME** to **838255** to connect with a volunteer Crisis Counselor.

About the Author

Dr. Tom Seals served in the United States Marine Corps from 1957-1960, with the 3rd Marine Division in Okinawa, Japan, during the Laos-Vietnam era, followed by several years with the U.S. Government in Europe.

Later, he taught undergraduate Bible courses as well as Biblical ethics and textual studies for twenty-eight years at Lipscomb University in Nashville, TN, and served as Chaplain to Veterans until his December 2020 retirement. He received the diploma, Master Course in Electronics from Cleveland Institute of Electronics in 1964, his Bachelor of Arts in Biblical languages from Lipscomb University in Nashville, TN, in 1971, his Master's degree from

Wesley Seminary in Washington, D.C. in 1976, and his Doctorate in Ministry from Memphis Theological Seminary in 1999. Dr. Seals later completed post-doctoral work in Pentateuchal Studies and Religion, Politics, and Social Issues from Vanderbilt University in 2008.

He has published *Proverbs: Wisdom for All Ages, Sermon on the Mount for Modern Living, The Quest for Spiritual Maturity: A Study of Dietrich Bonhoeffer's The Cost of Discipleship,* and *God's Word for Warriors.*

He has served as a pulpit minister in Virginia, Tennessee, and Colorado and is presently teaching at the Bellevue Church of Christ in Nashville, TN. Tom was actively involved with an educational ministry in Lima, Peru, serving as International President. Presently, Tom serves as Founder and President of God's Word for Warriors.

Tom and his wife, Barbara, have three children: Amy, Tom Jr. (deceased), and Melanie, along with three grandchildren.

Available online
wherever books are sold.

Contact the Author

contactus@godswordforwarriors.com

912 Harpeth Valley Place
Nashville, TN 37221

615.964.7450